LABORATORY MANUAL TO ACCOMPANY

Legal Issues in Information Security

VERSION 2.0

Powered by vLab Solutions

JONES & BARTLETT
LEARNING

World Headquarters
Jones & Bartlett Learning
5 Wall Street
Burlington, MA 01803
978-443-5000
info@jblearning.com
www.jblearning.com

Jones & Bartlett Learning books and products are available through most bookstores and online booksellers. To contact Jones & Bartlett Learning directly, call 800-832-0034, fax 978-443-8000, or visit our website, www.jblearning.com.

Substantial discounts on bulk quantities of Jones & Bartlett Learning publications are available to corporations, professional associations, and other qualified organizations. For details and specific discount information, contact the special sales department at Jones & Bartlett Learning via the above contact information or send an email to specialsales@jblearning.com.

Production Credits

Chief Executive Officer: Ty Field
President: James Homer
Chief Product Officer: Eduardo Moura
SVP, Curriculum Solutions: Christopher Will
Director of Sales, Curriculum Solutions: Randi Roger
Author: vLab Solutions, LLC, David Kim, President
Editorial Management: High Stakes Writing, LLC, Lawrence J. Goodrich, President
Copy Editor, High Stakes Writing: Katherine Dillin
Developmental Editor, High Stakes Writing: Dee Hayes

Associate Program Manager: Rainna Erikson
Production Manager: Susan Beckett
Rights & Photo Research Associate: Lauren Miller
Manufacturing and Inventory Control Supervisor: Amy Bacus
Senior Marketing Manager: Andrea DeFronzo
Cover Design: Scott Moden
Cover Image: © DVARG/ShutterStock, Inc.
Printing and Binding: Edwards Brothers Malloy
Cover Printing: Edwards Brothers Malloy

ISBN: 978-1-284-05870-3

6048

Printed in the United States of America

18 17 16   10 9 8 7 6 5 4 3 2

Contents

iv

Ethics and Your Personal Responsibilities

The material presented in this course is designed to give you a real-life look at the use of various tools and systems that are at the heart of every cybersecurity practitioner's daily responsibilities. During this course, you will have access to software and techniques used by professionals to investigate and test the security of critical infrastructures and information technology systems and devices. With this access come certain ethical responsibilities:

1. Do not exceed your authorized level of access. This includes remaining within your authorized level of access when using lab-provided software tools to scan or attack computers and software applications as directed within the lab procedures.

2. Do not attempt to use your authorized access for unauthorized purposes either inside or outside of the VSCL environment.

3. Do not attempt to attack or otherwise compromise the confidentiality, integrity, or availability of *any* IT systems, services, or infrastructures outside of the VSCL.

4. Comply with your academic institution's *Code of Student Conduct* and all other applicable policies and regulations.

5. Comply with applicable federal, state, and local laws regarding the use and misuse of information technology systems and services.

6. Comply with applicable laws regarding intellectual property rights, including patents and trademarks and copyrights.

Preface

Welcome! This lab manual is your step-by-step guide to completing the laboratory exercises for this course. You will have an opportunity to gain valuable hands-on experience with professional-grade tools and techniques as you work through the lab activities and answer the lab questions found at the end of each lab.

How to Use This Lab Manual

This lab manual features step-by-step instructions for completing the following hands-on lab exercises:

Lab #	Lab Title
1	Creating an IT Infrastructure Asset List and Identifying Where Privacy Data Resides
2	Case Study on U.S. Veterans Affairs and Loss of Privacy Information
3	Case Study on PCI DSS Noncompliance: CardSystems Solutions
4	Analyzing and Comparing GLBA and HIPAA
5	Case Study on Issues Related to Sharing Consumers' Confidential Information
6	Identifying the Scope of Your State's Data and Security Breach Notification Law
7	Case Study on Digital Millennium Copyright Act: Napster
8	Cyberstalking or Cyberbullying and Laws to Protect Individuals
9	Recommending IT Security Policies to Help Mitigate Risk
10	Case Study in Computer Forensics: Pharmaceutical Company

Step-by-Step Instructions

For each lab, you are provided with detailed, step-by-step instructions and screen captures showing the results of key steps within the lab. All actions that you are required to take are shown in **bold** font. The screen captures will also help you identify menus, dialog boxes, and input locations.

Deliverables

As you work through each lab, you will be instructed to record specific information or take a screen capture to document the results you obtained by performing specific actions. The deliverables are designed to test your understanding of the information, and your successful completion of the steps and functions of the lab. All of these documentation tasks should be pasted into a single file (MS Word .doc, .docx, or other compatible format) and submitted for grading by your instructor.

You will create two deliverable files for each lab:

- *Lab Report file* (including screen captures taken at specific steps in the lab)
- *Lab Assessment file* (including answers to questions posed at the end of each lab)

You may use either Microsoft® Word or any other compatible word processing software for these deliverables. For specific information on deliverables, refer to the Deliverables section in each lab.

Lab Assessment File

At the end of each lab, there is a set of questions which are to be answered and submitted for grading in the Lab Assessment file. (Your instructor may provide alternate instructions for this deliverable.) For some questions, you may need to refer to your Lab Report file to obtain information from the lab. For other questions, you may need to consult a textbook or other authoritative source to obtain more information.

Web References

URLs for Web resources listed in this laboratory manual are subject to change without prior notice. These links were last verified on April 13, 2014. Many times, you can find the required resource by using an Internet search engine and a partial URL or keywords. You may also search the Internet Archives (also referred to as the "Wayback Machine") for a given URL that is no longer available at the original Web site (http://www.archive.org).

Technical Support

If you need help completing a lab in this manual, contact the Jones & Bartlett Learning Help Desk using the information below. Remember to include the name of your institution and reference the course name and number in your ticket details

Phone: 1-866-601-4525

Online: http://www.jblcourses.com/techsupport

Monday-Thursday:	8AM – 10PM
Friday:	8AM – 8PM
Saturday:	8AM – 5PM
Sunday:	10AM – 11PM

(All hours are EST)

If you need help outside of these hours, submit an online ticket or leave a message on our toll-free phone line, and someone from the help desk will get back to you as soon as possible.

Credits

Adobe Reader® is a registered trademark of Adobe Systems Incorporated in the United States and/or other countries. Active Directory®, Excel®, Microsoft®, Windows®, and Windows Server® are registered trademarks of Microsoft Corporation in the United States and/or other countries. Linux® is a registered trademark of Linus Torvalds. Citrix® is a registered trademark of Citrix Systems, Inc. and/or one or more of its subsidiaries, and may be registered in the United States Patent and Trademark Office and in other countries. FileZilla® is a registered trademark of Tim Kosse. Firefox® is a registered trademark of the Mozilla Foundation. Nessus® is a registered trademark of Tenable Network Security. NetWitness® is a registered trademark of EMC Corporation in the United States and other countries. Nmap Security Scanner® and Zenmap® are either registered trademarks or trademarks of Insecure.com LLC. Wireshark® is a registered trademark of the Wireshark Foundation. pfSense® is a federally registered trademark of Electric Sheep Fencing LLC. Debian® is a registered trademark of Software in the Public Interest, Inc. Retina® is a registered trademark of BeyondTrust, Inc. Openswan® is an unregistered trademark of Xelerance.

All brand names and product names used in this document are trademarks, registered trademarks, or trade names of their respective holders.

Lab #1 Creating an IT Infrastructure Asset List and Identifying Where Privacy Data Resides

Introduction

Privacy is of growing concern, especially that of individual personal information. Between businesses seeking more effective use of their marketing budgets and governments targeting potential hostiles, the individual struggles to keep any information private.

The purpose of an IT asset identification and asset classification exercise is to protect privacy data and implement security controls. Identifying where privacy data is accessed throughout an IT infrastructure or outside of its protected environment is important.

In this lab, you will create an IT asset/inventory checklist organized within the seven domains of a typical IT infrastructure, you will perform an asset identification and classification exercise, you will explain how a data classification standard is linked to customer privacy data and security controls, and you will identify where privacy data resides and what security controls are needed to maintain compliance.

Learning Objectives

Upon completing this lab, you will be able to:

- Create an IT asset/inventory checklist organized within the seven domains of a typical IT infrastructure.
- Perform an asset identification and asset classification exercise for a typical IT infrastructure.
- Explain how a data classification standard is linked to customer privacy data protection and proper security controls.
- Identify where privacy data can reside or traverse throughout the seven domains of a typical IT infrastructure.
- Identify where privacy data protection and proper security controls are needed to assist organizations with maintaining compliance.

Deliverables

Upon completion of this lab, you are required to provide the following deliverables to your instructor:

1. Lab Report file;
2. Lab Assessments file.

Instructor Demo

The Instructor will present the instructions for this lab. This will start with a general discussion of asset identification and asset classification from a risk management perspective. The Instructor will then present an overview of the risks, threats, and vulnerabilities commonly found within the seven domains of a typical IT infrastructure.

Hands-On Steps

> **►Note:**
> This is a paper-based lab. To successfully complete the deliverables for this lab, you will need access to Microsoft®
> Word or another compatible word processor. For some labs, you may also need access to a graphics line drawing
> application, such as Visio or PowerPoint. Refer to the Preface of this manual for information on creating the lab
> deliverable files.

1. On your local computer, **create** the **lab deliverable files**.

2. **Review** the **Lab Assessment Worksheet**. You will find answers to these questions as you proceed through the lab steps.

3. **Review** the seven domains of a typical IT infrastructure.

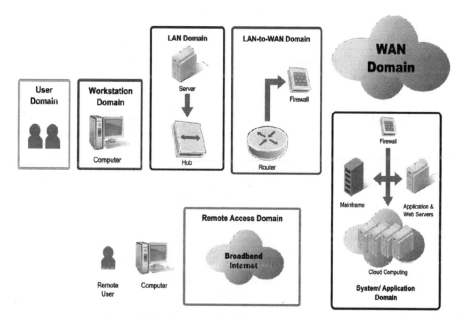

Figure 1 Seven domains of a typical IT infrastructure

An Asset's Finer Points
A domain is not the same as an asset. And a piece of hardware does not always equate to one asset. Many
assets can be in one domain, such as the System/Application Domain. A single hardware firewall might present
itself as two assets, one in two different domains, for example, a Local Area Network-to-Wide Area Network (LAN-
to-WAN) firewall and a Wide Area Network (WAN) firewall. In your own environments, ask yourself, "What function
does this perform?"

4. **Review** Figure 2, which is a Mock IT infrastructure with a Cisco core backbone network.

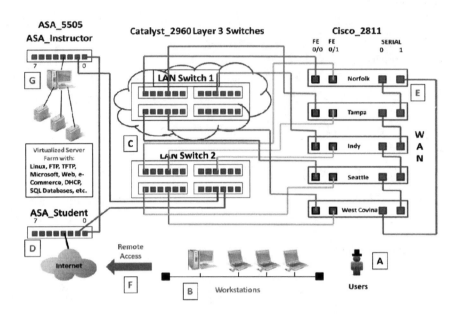

Figure 2 Mock IT infrastructure with Cisco core backbone network

5. **Refer** to Figure 2 and **note** the following information, which describes the details of the Workstation Domain and System/Application Domain at a health care provider under the Health Insurance Portability and Accountability Act (HIPAA) compliance law:

• Workstation Domain: Indicated by the "B" in Figure 2, the Workstation Domain consists of Microsoft® XP 2003, SP2 workstations (50), laptops (50), and desktop computers (50).

• System/Application Domain: Indicated by the "G" in Figure 2, the System/Application Domain consists of the following servers and applications:
   o Linux® Server #1 (Domain Name Server [DNS], File Transfer Protocol [FTP], and Trivial File Transfer Protocol [TFTP])
   o Linux® Server #2 (Web Server)
   o Microsoft® Server #1 (e-Commerce Server and Customer Database Subset)
   o Microsoft® Server #2 (Master Structured Query Language [SQL] Customer Database and Intellectual Property Assets)
   o Microsoft® Server #3 (Office Automation, Dynamic Host Configuration Protocol [DHCP] Server, and Customer Database Subset)
   o Microsoft® Server #4 (E-mail Server)

6. In your Lab Report file, use the following table to **identify** three to five IT assets and insert them into the table. **Indicate** in which of the seven domains of an IT infrastructure the asset resides. **Indicate** if the asset accesses customer privacy data or contains customer privacy data. Finally, **classify** the IT asset as Critical, Major, or Minor, where the following defines each:

- **Critical:** Generates revenues or represents intellectual property asset of organization
- **Major:** Contains customer privacy data
- **Minor:** Required for normal business functions and operations

IT Asset Description	Seven Domains of Typical IT	Privacy Data Impact	Assessment [Critical-Major-Minor]

> ▶ **Note:**
> Pay attention to the descriptions of the various System/Application assets. Individual assets may fall into different assessment categories. The same certainly holds true for real-world environments you will assess. The guiding question should always be "What does this asset do?" or "What sort of data does it hold?"

7. In your Lab Report file, **explain** how a data classification standard is related to customer privacy data protection and security controls.

> ▶ **Note:**
> This completes the lab. **Close** the **Web browser**, if you have not already done so.

Evaluation Criteria and Rubrics

The following are the evaluation criteria for this lab that students must perform:

1. Create an IT asset/inventory checklist organized within the seven domains of a typical IT infrastructure. – **[20%]**
2. Perform an asset identification and asset classification exercise for a typical IT infrastructure. – **[20%]**
3. Explain how a data classification standard is linked to customer privacy data protection and proper security controls. – **[20%]**
4. Identify where privacy data can reside or traverse throughout the seven domains of a typical IT infrastructure. – **[20%]**
5. Identify where privacy data protection and proper security controls are needed to assist organizations with maintaining compliance. – **[20%]**

Lab #1 - Assessment Worksheet

Creating an IT Infrastructure Asset List and Identifying Where Privacy Data Resides

Course Name and Number: _____

Student Name: _____

Instructor Name: _____

Lab Due Date: _____

Overview

In this lab, you created an IT asset/inventory checklist organized within the seven domains of a typical IT infrastructure, you performed an asset identification and classification exercise, you explained how a data classification standard is linked to customer privacy data and security controls, and you identified where privacy data resides and what security controls are needed to maintain compliance.

Lab Assessment Questions & Answers

1. What is the purpose of identifying IT assets and inventory?

2. What is the purpose of an asset classification?

3. Why might an organization's Web site classification be minor but its e-commerce server be considered critical for your scenario?

4. Why would you classify customer privacy data and intellectual property assets as critical?

5. What are some examples of security controls for recent compliance law requirements?

6. How can a data classification standard help with asset classification?

7. Given the importance of a Master SQL database that houses customer privacy data and intellectual property assets, what security controls and security countermeasures can you apply to help protect these assets?

8. From a legal and liability perspective, what recommendations do you have for ensuring the confidentiality of customer privacy data throughout the Mock IT infrastructure?

9. What can your organization document and implement to help mitigate the risks, threats, and liabilities typically found in an IT infrastructure?

10. True or false: Organizations under recent compliancy laws, such as HIPAA and the Gramm-Leach-Bliley Act (GLBA), are mandated to have documented IT security policies, standards, procedures, and guidelines.

11. Why is it important to identify where privacy data resides throughout your IT infrastructure?

Lab #2 Case Study on U.S. Veterans Affairs and Loss of Privacy Information

Introduction

Privacy is not something to take for granted as true privacy becomes increasingly challenging to find. In most day-to-day cases, you are aware that your information is being collected. As you drive, video surveillance monitors for traffic conditions. When you purchase items with credit cards, your buying history is analyzed for marketing. As you use the Internet at work, your browsing habits might be monitored for performance. These are known impacts on personal privacy, but there are many other examples where your privacy is lost without your knowledge or consent.

The loss of privacy data has implications for both the individual(s) responsible and the organization at which the individual(s) works. Privacy and information systems security can be violated, but breaches can also be prevented.

In this lab, you will review a real-world case study that involves the loss of privacy information, and you will analyze what violations occurred, the implications of those violations, and the possible mitigation remedies that can prevent future violations.

Learning Objectives

Upon completing this lab, you will be able to:

- Relate a real-world case study on privacy law violation and its implications to the individual and the organization in violation.
- Distinguish how privacy law is different from information systems security.
- Review a case study on a U.S. government agency's loss of privacy data and information.
- Suggest possible mitigation remedies to prevent the same loss from occurring at another organization.

9

Deliverables

Upon completion of this lab, you are required to provide the following deliverables to your instructor:

1. Lab Report file;
2. Lab Assessments file.

Instructor Demo

The Instructor will present the instructions for this lab. This will start with a general discussion about privacy law and how this is different from, yet related to, information systems security. The Instructor will then present an overview of the U.S. Veterans Affairs' privacy loss breach and the case study lab exercise.

Hands-On Steps

> **▶Note:**
> This is a paper-based lab. To successfully complete the deliverables for this lab, you will need access to Microsoft® Word or another compatible word processor. For some labs, you may also need access to a graphics line drawing application, such as Visio or PowerPoint. Refer to the Preface of this manual for information on creating the lab deliverable files.

1. On your local computer, **create** the **lab deliverable files**.

2. **Review** the **Lab Assessment Worksheet**. You will find answers to these questions as you proceed through the lab steps.

3. **Review** the following **case study on U.S. Veterans Affairs and loss of privacy information**:

The U.S. Department of Veterans Affairs had a privacy data breach in 2006 that an agency employee said affected the records of 26.5 million veterans and their spouses. An employee at the agency reported the breach and said that a laptop he used at his home in Montgomery County, Maryland, had been stolen. This employee had been taking home a laptop that contained private information of the approximately 26.5 million veterans. This privacy information included the veterans' names, Social Security numbers, the dates of birth, and disability ratings.

On May 17, 2006, the Federal Bureau of Investigation (FBI) was informed of the breach, and it began an investigation along with the Veterans Affairs (VA) Inspector General's Office. During the investigation, it was discovered that more than the originally reported veterans and their spouses were affected by the theft. In fact, approximately 1.1 million active-duty military personnel were affected, as well as 430,000 members of the National Guard and 645,000 members of the Reserves. In addition, the investigation revealed other information, including:

- On May 3, 2006, the theft occurred. The employee whose laptop was stolen reported the theft to his supervisors at the agency and to the Maryland police.
- On May 16, 2006, Veterans Affairs Secretary R. James Nicholson was told of the breach that resulted in unencrypted data being stolen. Supervisors at the agency knew of the theft on May 3 when it happened, but they failed to tell Mr. Nicholson until the May 16 date.
- On May 22, 2006, the agency finally informed those who were affected by the breach. The agency announced that the laptop had been stolen. The agency reported that the information stolen included veterans' and their spouses' names, Social Security numbers, birth dates, and disability ratings. The agency said that the information did not include financial data or electronic health records.

- The analyst who took the laptop home had been given permission to use the laptop at home. (The agency did not reveal this until after it had already said that the employee was fired for taking the laptop home.) The employee said that he had taken the laptop home regularly for three years.

Congress held a hearing on May 25, 2006. During this hearing, Secretary Nicholson admitted that the stolen information included disability ratings for 2.6 million people.

On June 3, the agency admitted that approximately 50,000 active-duty personnel were also affected by the stolen data. By June 6, 2006, the agency had admitted that approximately 1.1 million active-duty military personnel were affected, as well as 430,000 members of the National Guard and 645,000 members of the Reserves.

On June 29, 2006, an unidentified person turned the laptop over to the agency, which believes it will cost $100 million to $500 million to cover the data theft losses and prevent additional losses.

Calculating Costs

The concluding paragraph of this case study shows how difficult it can be to calculate the consequences of a crime. Violating data privacy is no exception. The range of $100 million to $500 million is by a factor of five! Why is the total so unclear?

Some costs directly relate to recovery from the crime, while other costs come from closing the vulnerabilities that allowed the crime to happen. The latter helps prevent the same crime from occurring again. It's easy for someone to simply decide the vulnerabilities should have been closed earlier, saving the recovery costs.

Of course, it's not that simple in real life. Without the gift of hindsight, costs are far less justified before a disaster than after. The powers that be will resist spending funds on any risk except the most probable and with the most serious consequences. It's not feasible to mitigate all identified risks, let alone identify and assess the unforeseen ones before they occur. So, some closure doesn't happen until after a risk presents itself in the worst way.

Still, why so different an estimate of consequential costs? The easier costs include money spent to fix the problem, appease those affected, and estimated losses from downtime. Those directly relate to the crime and are fairly quantifiable. Then additional costs stem from situations that might or might not happen, for example, identity theft and any resulting fraud. No one can calculate for certain that X percentage of the personnel will experience identity theft, or find out years later of a fraudulent loan. The guesswork involved helps broaden the costs, even if by a factor of five.

---

4. On your local computer, **open** a new **Internet browser window**.

5. In the address box of your Internet browser, **type** the URL **http://www.pcworld.com/article/126093/article.html** and **press Enter** to open the Web site.

6. **Read** and **review** Grant Gross's online article (IDG News Service), "VA Ignores Cybersecurity Warnings."

7. In your Lab Report file, **discuss** the case study and **answer** the following questions:

   - What laws have been violated?
   - What do you think contributed to the problems that could lead to a violation of these laws?
   - What are the implications to the individual and organization of these violations?
   - What are some security controls and mitigation strategies for handling future violations? (Name three to five.)
   - How does privacy law differ from information systems security?

Evaluation Criteria and Rubrics

The following are the evaluation criteria for this lab that students must perform:

1. Relate a real-world case study on privacy law violation and its implications to the individual and the organization in violation. – **[25%]**
2. Distinguish how privacy law is different from information systems security. – **[25%]**
3. Review a case study on a U.S. government agency's loss of privacy data and information. – **[25%]**
4. Suggest possible mitigation remedies to prevent the same loss from occurring at another organization. – **[25%]**

Lab #2 - Assessment Worksheet

Case Study on U.S. Veterans Affairs and Loss of Privacy Information

Course Name and Number: _____

Student Name: _____

Instructor Name: _____

Lab Due Date: _____

Overview

In this lab, you reviewed a real-world case study that involved the loss of privacy information, and you analyzed what violations occurred, the implications of those violations, and the possible mitigation remedies that could prevent future violations.

Lab Assessment Questions & Answers

1. What is the difference between privacy law and information systems security? How are they related?

2. Was the employee justified in taking home official data? Why or why not?

3. What are the possible consequences associated with the data loss?

4. Regarding the loss of privacy data, was there any data containing protected health information (PHI) making this a Health Insurance Portability and Accountability Act (HIPAA) compliance violation?

5. What action can the agency take against the employee concerned?

6. Would the response of the agency have been different had the data theft occurred at work instead of happening at the employee's residence? Why or why not?

7. Why were the VA data analyst's two supervisors reprimanded and demoted by the VA secretary? Do you think this was justified? Why or why not?

8. What was violated in this data breach?

9. If the database had been encrypted because of VA policy, would this data loss issue even have been an issue? Why or why not?

10. What risk mitigation or security control recommendations would you suggest to prevent this from occurring again?

11. What information systems security and privacy security policies do you think would help mitigate this breach and loss of privacy data?

12. What or who was the weakest link in this chain of security and protection of privacy data?

13. If the VA had performed a security and information assurance audit for compliance, what could the VA do on an annual basis to help mitigate this type of loose policy conformance?

14. True or false: U.S. taxpayers ended up paying for this VA security breach, notifications, and post-mortem damage control.

15. Which organization in the U.S. federal government is responsible for performing audits on other U.S. federal government agencies? (Hint: It is also known as the "Congressional Watchdog.")

Lab #3 Case Study on PCI DSS Noncompliance: CardSystems Solutions

Introduction

Payment Card Industry Data Security Standard (PCI DSS) is a compliance standard that helps prevent private data breaches in companies. Before PCI DSS was drafted, each credit card company had its own security requirements. Any merchant wanting to accept that company's credit card would need to comply with the company's security requirements. Merchants wanting to accept multiple credit cards grew frustrated by having to comply with multiple sets of requirements. To assist merchants, card companies sought a solution.

The solution began with the major credit card companies collaborating to form a representative group, now called the PCI Security Standards Council. Commonly called the PCI Council, they drafted and approved the standard, the PCI DSS. It's important to remember that the PCI Council is a group of companies, not a government agency. While the PCI Council is a group, only the individual credit card company can enforce PCI DSS on its own card. Instances of noncompliance are dealt with through penalties.

In this lab, you will review a real-world case study that involves a PCI DSS noncompliance scenario, and you will recommend mitigation remedies to prevent the loss of private data for similar organizations.

Learning Objectives

Upon completing this lab, you will be able to:

- Relate a real-world case study on the Payment Card Industry Data Security Standard (PCI DSS) standard noncompliance and its implications.
- Distinguish how the Payment Card Industry Data Security Standard (PCI DSS) is a standard and not a law, and how it defines requirements for information systems security controls and countermeasures.
- Review a case study on a credit card transaction-processing company's noncompliance with the Payment Card Industry Data Security Standard (PCI DSS) and identify the privacy data breach that occurred.
- Recommend PCI DSS-compliant mitigation remedies to prevent the same loss from occurring again at a similar organization.

Deliverables

Upon completion of this lab, you are required to provide the following deliverables to your instructor:

1. Lab Report file;
2. Lab Assessments file.

Instructor Demo

The Instructor will present the instructions for this lab. This will start with a general discussion about the PCI DSS standard and the required security controls and security countermeasures that the standard defines. PCI DSS is a standard, not a law. PCI DSS directly impacts information systems security given that it defines requirements. The Instructor will then present an overview of the case study in this lab.

Hands-On Steps

> ▶ **Note:**
> This is a paper-based lab. To successfully complete the deliverables for this lab, you will need access to Microsoft® Word or another compatible word processor. For some labs, you may also need access to a graphics line drawing application, such as Visio or PowerPoint. Refer to the Preface of this manual for information on creating the lab deliverable files.

1. On your local computer, **create** the **lab deliverable files**.

2. **Review** the **Lab Assessment Worksheet**. You will find answers to these questions as you proceed through the lab steps.

3. **Review** the Payment Card Industry Data Security Standard (PCI DSS) overview in Figure 1.

PCI Data Security Standard—High-Level Overview
Build and Maintain a Secure Network
Requirement 1: Install and maintain a firewall configuration to protect cardholder data.
Requirement 2: Do not use vendor-supplied defaults for system passwords and other security parameters.
Protect Cardholder Data
Requirement 3: Protect stored cardholder data.
Requirement 4: Encrypt transmission of cardholder data across open, public networks.
Maintain a Vulnerability Management Program
Requirement 5: Use and regularly update antivirus software.
Requirement 6: Develop and maintain secure systems and applications.
Implement Strong Access Control Measures
Requirement 7: Restrict access to cardholder data by business need-to-know.
Requirement 8: Assign a unique ID to each person with computer access.
Requirement 9: Restrict physical access to cardholder data.
Regularly Monitor and Test Networks

Requirement 10: Track and monitor all access to network resources and cardholder data.
Requirement 11: Regularly test security systems and processes.
Maintain an Information Security Policy
Requirement 12: Maintain a policy that addresses information security.

Figure 1 PCI DSS v1.2 information systems security requirements

4. In your Lab Report file, **explain** how PCI DSS is a standard and not a law and **discuss** how it defines requirements for information systems security controls and countermeasures.

▶**Note:**
Upon review of the PCI DSS supporting documents repository (link provided in below step), you will see a "Prioritized Approach v2.0" document. This document details the 12 requirements of PCI DSS and prioritizes them in a to-do list resembling a Gantt chart. Highly recommended.

5. **Review** the following case study on PCI DSS noncompliance:

External hackers managed to breach a credit card transaction-processing firm, resulting in the theft of privacy information. You can find more information on this case against the company, CardSystems Solutions, by visiting the Federal Trade Commission's (FTC's) Web site at *http://www.ftc.gov/news-events/press-releases/2006/02/cardsystems-solutions-settles-ftc-charges*. You can find information about the PCI DSS standard and PCI DSS requirements documents by visiting *https://www.pcisecuritystandards.org/security_standards/pci_dss_supporting_docs.shtml*

Case Study: CardSystems Solutions

CardSystems Solutions, a third-party payment processor, collected thousands of transactions of small and medium businesses. These transactions were then processed as batches and sent to credit card providers (such as Visa and MasterCard). The company's collection and processing of private information and financial data made it a prime target of potential hackers. Because of this, the company had to meet the data security standards that the federal, state, and industry standards require. Compliance is not optional for companies such as CardSystems Solutions.

In June 2004, an external auditor certified the company as Payment Card Industry Data Security Standard- (PCI DSS-) compliant. The PCI DSS standards include installing a firewall and antivirus software and updating virus definitions on a consistent schedule. Companies must also encrypt privacy data elements. The company's certification implied that it followed a high standard of security, meaning the company used encryption methods to store privacy data. However, after the breach, a security assessment was conducted. This assessment of the security measures used at the company proved that the company was not PCI DSS-compliant.

The hacker who performed the attack used a basic exploit known as a Structured Query Language (SQL) injection, which allows the hacker to place a snippet of code into the application. The hacker gained access through a Web application that customers used to access their data. With the code inserted into the fields of a form, the hacker was able to send SQL commands to the backend SQL server. The hacker wrote a script that gathered credit card data from the database, put it in a compressed ZIP file, and sent the credit card data to the hacker community through a File Transfer Protocol (FTP) site. The impact of the attack almost caused the company to go out of business. It had to eventually be acquired by another business.

These types of SQL injection attacks can be mitigated. Quality Web site design, secure coding, and internal firewalls all contribute to mitigating these types of attacks. The PCI DSS standard requires these types of mitigation controls and security methods. CardSystems was supposedly in compliance with the PCI DSS standard; however, if the company were in compliance, a successful SQL injection attack would mean the firewall was somehow circumvented.

> **▶ Note:**
> Implementing PCI DSS controls will not prevent the most determined hacker from successfully attacking, but they provide a calculated level of due diligence to close virtually all attack channels.

CardSystems stored unencrypted data and failed to use proper security firewalls. It also failed to maintain its antivirus definitions. As a result, the FTC found CardSystems Solutions and its predecessors negligent and in violation of the FTC Act 15, U.S.C. §§ 41-58.

Federal Trade Commission Act (15 U.S.C. §§ 41-58, as amended)

Under this act, the commission is empowered, among other things, to (a) prevent unfair methods of competition and unfair or deceptive acts or practices in or affecting commerce; (b) seek monetary redress and other relief for conduct injurious to consumers; (c) prescribe trade regulation rules defining with specificity acts or practices that are unfair or deceptive, and establishing requirements designed to prevent such acts or practices; (d) conduct investigations relating to the organization, business, practices, and management of entities engaged in commerce; and (e) make reports and legislative recommendations to Congress.

6. In your Lab Report file, **discuss** the PCI DSS requirements related to the case study on PCI DSS noncompliance. **Explain** which requirements weren't met and how these violate the Federal Trade Commission Act.

7. In your Lab Report file, **recommend** two or three mitigation remedies to prevent the same thing from happening at another organization.

> ▶ **Note:**
> This completes the lab. **Close** the **Web browser**, if you have not already done so.

Evaluation Criteria and Rubrics

The following are the evaluation criteria for this lab that students must perform:

1. Relate a real-world case study on the Payment Card Industry Data Security Standard (PCI DSS) standard noncompliance and its implications. – **[25%]**
2. Distinguish how the Payment Card Industry Data Security Standard (PCI DSS) is a standard and not a law, and how it defines requirements for information systems security controls and countermeasures. – **[25%]**
3. Review a case study on a credit card transaction-processing company's noncompliance with the Payment Card Industry Data Security Standard (PCI DSS) and identify the privacy data breach that occurred. – **[25%]**
4. Recommend PCI DSS-compliant mitigation remedies to prevent the same loss from occurring again at a similar organization. – **[25%]**

Lab #3 - Assessment Worksheet

Case Study on PCI DSS Noncompliance: CardSystems Solutions

Course Name and Number: _____

Student Name: _____

Instructor Name: _____

Lab Due Date: _____

Overview

In this lab, you reviewed a real-world case study that involved a PCI DSS noncompliance scenario, and you recommended mitigation remedies to prevent the loss of private data for similar organizations.

Lab Assessment Questions & Answers

1. Did CardSystems Solutions break any federal or state laws?

2. In June 2004, an external auditor certified CardSystems Solutions as Payment Card Industry Data Security Standard- (PCI DSS-) compliant. What is your assessment of the auditor's findings?

3. Can CardSystems Solutions sue the auditor for not performing his or her tasks and deliverables with accuracy? Do you recommend that CardSystems Solutions pursue this avenue?

4. Who do you think is negligent in this case study and why?

5. Do the actions of CardSystems Solutions warrant an "unfair trade practice" designation as stated by the Federal Trade Commission (FTC)?

6. What security policies do you recommend to help with monitoring, enforcing, and ensuring PCI DSS compliance?

7. What security controls and security countermeasures do you recommend for CardSystems Solutions to be in compliance with PCI DSS requirements?

8. What was the end result of the attack and security breach to CardSystems Solutions and its valuation?

9. What are the possible consequences associated with the data loss?

10. Who do you think is ultimately responsible for CardSystems Solutions' lack of PCI DSS compliance?

11. What should CardSystems Solutions have done to mitigate possible SQL injections and data breaches on its credit card transaction-processing engine?

12. True or false: Although CardSystems Solutions had proper security controls and security countermeasures, it was not 100 percent PCI DSS-compliant because the company failed to properly implement ongoing monitoring and testing on its development and production systems.

Lab #4 Analyzing and Comparing GLBA and HIPAA

Introduction

Individuals and customers should normally expect companies and health providers to protect personal information. Custodians of private information should protect it as they would any other asset. Personal information has great market value both to other companies and would-be thieves. Because of this value, numerous examples exist of companies opting to share, sell, or inadequately safeguard their customers' personal information. The result has been two landmark pieces of legislation.

The purpose of the Gramm-Leach-Bliley Act (GLBA) and the Health Insurance Portability and Accountability Act (HIPAA) is to make organizations responsible and accountable for protecting customer privacy data and implementing security controls to mitigate risks, threats, and vulnerabilities of that data. Both of these laws impact their industries significantly.

In this lab, you will identify the similarities and differences of GLBA and HIPAA compliance laws, you will explain how the requirements of GLBA and HIPAA align with information systems security, you will identify privacy data elements for each, and you will describe security controls and countermeasures that support each.

Learning Objectives

Upon completing this lab, you will be able to:

- Identify the similarities between GLBA and HIPAA compliance laws.
- Identify the differences between GLBA and HIPAA compliance laws.
- Explain how GLBA and HIPAA requirements align with information systems security.
- Identify privacy data elements for both GLBA and HIPAA.
- Describe specific security controls and security countermeasures that support GLBA and HIPAA compliance.

27

Deliverables

Upon completion of this lab, you are required to provide the following deliverables to your instructor:

1. Lab Report file;
2. Lab Assessments file.

Instructor Demo

The Instructor will present the instructions for this lab. This will start with a general discussion about GLBA and HIPAA, their similarities, differences, etc. The Instructor will then present an overview of this lab and reference the overview documents.

Hands-On Steps

> **▶Note:**
> This is a paper-based lab. To successfully complete the deliverables for this lab, you will need access to Microsoft® Word or another compatible word processor. For some labs, you may also need access to a graphics line drawing application, such as Visio or PowerPoint. Refer to the Preface of this manual for information on creating the lab deliverable files.

1. On your local computer, **create** the **lab deliverable files**.

2. **Review** the **Lab Assessment Worksheet**. You will find answers to these questions as you proceed through the lab steps.

3. On your local computer, **open** a new **Internet browser window**.

4. Using your favorite search engine, **search for information** on the **Gramm-Leach-Bliley Act.**

5. **Read** about this act.

6. Next, **research** the **privacy and security rules** for the Gramm-Leach-Bliley Act.

7. In your Lab Report file, **write** a thorough description of the Gramm-Leach-Bliley Act's basic components. Be sure to include the following topics:

   • Who co-sponsored the act?
   • Who is protected by the act?
   • Who is restricted by the act?
   • How are financial institutions defined?
   • What does the act allow?
   • How would you define the major parts of the privacy requirements: the Financial Privacy Rule, the Safeguards Rule, and the pretexting provisions? What do each of these spell out in the act? (**Write** three paragraphs on each of these.)

8. Using your favorite search engine, **research** the compliance law **HIPAA.**

9. In your Lab Report file, **write** a thorough description of HIPAA. Be sure to include the following topics in your discussion:

   • Which U.S. government agency acts as the legal enforcement entity for HIPAA compliance violations?
   • Who is protected by HIPAA?
   • Who must comply with HIPAA?
   • What is the relevance of health care plans, providers, and clearinghouses?

- How would you define the major parts of the Privacy Rule and the Security Rule? What do each of these spell out? (**Write** three paragraphs on each rule.)

10. In your Lab Report file, **describe** what the GLBA and HIPAA **privacy rules** have in common. Then, **discuss** how the two are different.

11. In your Lab Report file, **describe** what the GLBA and HIPAA **security rules** have in common. Then, **discuss** how the two are different.

Historical Differences Between GLBA and HIPAA

GLBA and HIPAA offer up historical similarities and differences. Both acts were drafted and made into law only a few years apart, with HIPAA in 1996 and GLBA in 1999. And both acts tackled gaps in information assurance and privacy, and are constructed similarly. However, HIPAA's Privacy Rule and Security Rule were published by the U.S. Department of Health and Human Services some four and seven years, respectively, after the act's passage. GLBA's Privacy Rule and Safeguards Rule were drafted alongside the original act.

Both acts target their particular industries with rules and control measures to protect information. However, each act's impact is limited based on where most of its industry is located. For instance, health care providers covered by HIPAA's mandate to protect information operate within the United States. By contrast, many large banks have locations and headquarters all over the globe, not just within the United States. But GLBA is enforceable only in the United States.

Yet another notable difference between the two acts is how dominant the issue of information confidentiality is to each act. HIPAA has two purposes: to help individuals retain health insurance and to help them control their personal data. GLBA's primary purpose is unrelated to information assurance altogether. Rather, GLBA was enacted to repeal many restrictions and regulations placed on banks from the Glass-Steagall Act of 1933. Once GLBA was in place, banks were free to consolidate and quickly grow without hindrance from any financial regulatory agency. In fact, popular opinion is that GLBA allowed banks to become "too big to fail," a phrase coined during the losing argument against GLBA in 1999. Consequently, history was made in 2007 with the U.S. financial crisis. But GLBA also ensured the banks would safeguard personal information.

12. In your Lab Report file, **discuss** how GLBA and HIPAA requirements align with information systems security.

13. In you Lab Report file, **list** two privacy data elements for GLBA and **list** two privacy data elements for HIPAA that are under compliance.

14. In your Lab Report file, **list** two security controls or security countermeasures for GLBA and **list** two security controls or security countermeasures for HIPAA that support compliance.

▶ Note:
This completes the lab. **Close** the **Web browser**, if you have not already done so.

Evaluation Criteria and Rubrics

The following are the evaluation criteria for this lab that students must perform:

1. Identify the similarities between GLBA and HIPAA compliance laws. – **[20%]**
2. Identify the differences between GLBA and HIPAA compliance laws. – **[20%]**
3. Explain how GLBA and HIPAA requirements align with information systems security. – **[20%]**
4. Identify privacy data elements for both GLBA and HIPAA. – **[20%]**
5. Describe specific security controls and security countermeasures that support GLBA and HIPAA compliance. – **[20%]**

Lab #4 - Assessment Worksheet

Analyzing and Comparing GLBA and HIPAA

Course Name and Number: _____

Student Name: _____

Instructor Name: _____

Lab Due Date: _____

Overview

In this lab, you identified the similarities and differences of GLBA and HIPAA compliance laws, you explained how the requirements of GLBA and HIPAA align with information systems security, you identified privacy data elements for each, and you described security controls and countermeasures that support each.

Lab Assessment Questions & Answers

1. Which U.S. government agency acts as the legal enforcement entity for businesses and organizations involved in commerce?

2. Which U.S. government agency acts as the legal enforcement entity regarding HIPAA compliance and HIPAA violations?

3. List three (3) similarities between GLBA and HIPAA.

4. List five (5) examples of privacy data elements for GLBA as defined in the Financial Privacy Rule.

5. List five (5) examples of privacy data elements for HIPAA as defined in the Privacy Rule.

6. List three (3) differences between GLBA and HIPAA.

7. How does GLBA's and HIPAA's privacy rule translate into information systems security controls and countermeasures?

8. What three areas does the GLBA Safeguards Rule encompass?

9. What is ePHI?

10. What three areas does the HIPAA Security Rule encompass for PHI?

11. Are organizations under GLBA and HIPAA required to mail and inform their customers in writing about their privacy rights?

12. When you go to your doctor's office, one of the forms the office asks you to fill in and sign is a HIPAA Release Form authorizing your doctor to share your medical records and privacy data with third parties, including health insurance companies. Is this an example of the HIPAA Privacy Rule or the HIPAA Security Rule?

13. Why is a Business Associate Agreement/Contract required between a HIPAA-covered entity and a downstream medical or service provider to that covered entity?

14. Like HIPAA, GLBA has both privacy and security rules. What are the official names of these rules in GLBA law?

15. True or false: GLBA encompasses insurance companies and stock brokerage firms.

Lab #5 Case Study on Issues Related to Sharing Consumers' Confidential Information

Introduction

When consumers provide personal information for a product or service, the assumption is the receiving company will exercise due diligence to protect their information. Bear in mind there is no all-purpose federal law mandating personal data should be protected, only certain industry-specific laws, for example, health care and financial. But even without an overarching mandate, most companies will attempt to protect your personal data just to avoid a charge of negligence should a privacy breach occur.

One nonprofit organization that monitors how well companies guard personal data—among other missions—is the Electronic Frontier Foundation (EFF). EFF's purpose is to defend free speech, privacy, innovation, and consumer rights. This lab takes a look at a class-action lawsuit filed by EFF.

In this lab, you will explain the privacy issues related to an EFF case study, you will identify U.S. privacy law violations and their implications, and you will assess the impact of those violations on consumer confidential information.

Learning Objectives

Upon completing this lab, you will be able to:

- Explain the mission statement of the Electronic Frontier Foundation (EFF).
- Relate privacy issues in the case study to any personal or individual laws in the United States.
- Identify U.S. citizen privacy law violations and their implications for privacy and confidential information in the case study.
- Assess the impact of these violations on consumers' confidential information from a legal, ethical, and information systems security perspective.

Deliverables

Upon completion of this lab, you are required to provide the following deliverables to your instructor:

1. Lab Report file;
2. Lab Assessments file.

Instructor Demo

The Instructor will present the instructions for this lab. This will start with a general discussion about privacy law and how this is different from information systems security as well as how they are related. The Instructor will then present an overview of the Electronic Frontier Foundation (EFF) and the case study in this lab.

Hands-On Steps

> ▶**Note:**
> This is a paper-based lab. To successfully complete the deliverables for this lab, you will need access to Microsoft® Word or another compatible word processor. For some labs, you may also need access to a graphics line drawing application, such as Visio or PowerPoint. Refer to the Preface of this manual for information on creating the lab deliverable files.

1. On your local computer, **create** the **lab deliverable files**.

2. **Review** the **Lab Assessment Worksheet**. You will find answers to these questions as you proceed through the lab steps.

3. **Review** the following case study on issues related to sharing consumers' confidential information (note that this information originated from the following Electronic Frontier Foundation Web pages: *https://www.eff.org/about*, *https://www.eff.org/cases/hepting*, and *https://www.eff.org/nsa/hepting*):

   From the Internet to the iPod, technologies transform society and empower us as speakers, citizens, creators, and consumers. When freedoms in the networked world come under attack, the Electronic Frontier Foundation (EFF) is the first line of defense. EFF broke new ground when it was founded in 1990—well before the Internet was on most people's radar—and continues to confront cutting-edge issues defending free speech, privacy, innovation, and consumer rights today. From the beginning, EFF has championed the public interest in every critical battle affecting digital rights.

   Blending the expertise of lawyers, policy analysts, activists, and technologists, EFF achieves significant victories on behalf of consumers and the general public. EFF fights for freedom primarily in the courts, bringing and defending lawsuits even when that means taking on the U.S. government or large corporations. By mobilizing more than 61,000 concerned citizens through the Action Center, EFF beats back bad legislation. In addition to advising policymakers, EFF educates the press and public.

   EFF is a donor-funded nonprofit and depends on support to continue successfully defending digital rights. Litigation is particularly expensive. Because two-thirds of EFF's budget comes from individual donors, every contribution is critical to helping EFF fight—and win—more cases (*https://www.eff.org/about*).

   EFF Case Study Information

   The Electronic Frontier Foundation (EFF) filed a class-action lawsuit against AT&T on January 31, 2006, accusing the telecom giant of violating the law and the privacy of its customers by collaborating with the National Security Agency (NSA) in its massive, illegal program to wiretap and data-mine Americans' communications. In May 2006, many other cases were filed against a variety of telecommunications companies. Subsequently, the Multi-District Litigation Panel of the federal courts transferred approximately 40 cases to the Northern District of California federal court.

In Hepting v. AT&T, EFF sued the telecommunications giant on behalf of its customers for violating privacy law by collaborating with the NSA in the massive, illegal program to wiretap and data-mine Americans' communications. Evidence in the case includes undisputed evidence provided by former AT&T telecommunications technician Mark Klein showing AT&T routed copies of Internet traffic to a secret room in San Francisco controlled by the NSA.

In June of 2009, a federal judge dismissed Hepting and dozens of other lawsuits against telecoms, ruling that the companies had immunity from liability under the controversial Foreign Intelligence Surveillance Act Amendments Act (FISAAA), which was enacted in response to court victories in Hepting. Signed by President Bush in 2008, the FISAAA allows the attorney general to require the dismissal of the lawsuits over the telecoms' participation in the warrantless surveillance program if the government secretly certifies to the court that the surveillance did not occur, was legal, or was authorized by the president—certification that was filed in September of 2008.

> ▶**Note:**
> To read the full order from the federal judge who dismissed the many EFF lawsuits, the order is available here: *http://www.eff.org/files/filenode/att/orderhepting6309_0.pdf.*

EFF plans to appeal the decision to the 9th U.S. Circuit Court of Appeals, primarily arguing that FISAAA is unconstitutional in granting to the president broad discretion to block the courts from considering the core constitutional privacy claims of millions of Americans (*http://www.eff.org/cases/hepting*; *https://www.eff.org/nsa/hepting*).

> ▶**Note:**
> Public proof regarding the case study came in June 2013 when British newspaper The Guardian first published news of massive electronic data collection by the NSA, a U.S. spy agency. Revelations from former NSA contractor and whistleblower Edward Snowden have detailed the extensiveness of data collection.

4. In your Lab Report file, **describe** the EFF's mission statement.

5. In your Lab Report file, **explain** the privacy issues in the case study.

6. In your Lab Report file, **identify** the U.S. citizen privacy law violations in the case study and the implications those violations have on privacy and confidential information.

> ▶**Note:**
> This completes the lab. **Close** the **Web browser**, if you have not already done so.

Evaluation Criteria and Rubrics

The following are the evaluation criteria for this lab that students must perform:

1. Explain the mission statement of the Electronic Frontier Foundation (EFF). – **[25%]**
2. Relate privacy issues in the case study to any personal or individual laws in the United States. – **[25%]**
3. Identify U.S. citizen privacy law violations and their implications for privacy and confidential information in the case study. – **[25%]**
4. Assess the impact of these violations on consumers' confidential information from a legal, ethical, and information systems security perspective. – **[25%]**

Lab #5 - Assessment Worksheet

Case Study on Issues Related to Sharing Consumers' Confidential Information

Course Name and Number: _____

Student Name: _____

Instructor Name: _____

Lab Due Date: _____

Overview

In this lab, you explained the privacy issues related to an EFF case study, you identified U.S. privacy law violations and their implications, and you assessed the impact of those violations on consumer confidential information.

Lab Assessment Questions & Answers

1. What is the Electronic Frontier Foundation's mission statement?

2. Did the U.S. government violate the constitutional rights of U.S. citizens by ordering the NSA to review consumer confidential privacy information?

3. Why is the Hepting v. AT&T case crucial to the long-term posture of how the U.S. government can or cannot review consumer confidential information?

4. If Hepting v. AT&T results in "Big Brother" being allowed to eavesdrop and/or review the local and toll telephone dialing and bills of individuals, will U.S. citizens and consumers have any privacy rights left regarding use of communication technologies?

5. What are the legal implications of consumer privacy information being shared?

6. What are the ethical implications of consumer privacy information being shared?

7. What are the information systems security implications of consumer information being shared?

8. What law allowed a federal judge to dismiss Hepting v. AT&T and other lawsuits against telecommunication service providers participating in the warrantless surveillance program authorized by the president?

9. True or false: EFF claimed that the ruling set forth by FISAAA was unconstitutional.

Lab #6 Identifying the Scope of Your State's Data and Security Breach Notification Law

Introduction

The United States does not have a unified data privacy law at the national level as, for example, many countries in Europe do. Laws such as the Health Insurance Portability and Accountability Act (HIPAA) and Gramm-Leach-Bliley Act (GLBA) are comprehensive and effective, but only protect consumers in a single industry.

So, what if an individual's private data is subjected to a security breach not covered by HIPAA or GLBA? Without an overarching federal mandate in effect, a company that discovered its data had been compromised is not compelled to notify all the affected individuals. Notification, and possible liability to provide identity theft protection, comes only in laws including mandated security breach notifications. To bridge the gap in privacy protection, most states have enacted their own privacy laws.

With the help of the Internet, you can research these gaps and find out what your state does to protect your privacy. For instance, the purpose of the National Conference of State Legislatures (NCSL) is, according to its Web site, to provide "access to current state and federal legislation and a comprehensive list of state documents, including state statutes, constitutions, legislative audits, and research reports."

In this lab, you will review the data security breach notification laws for your state and you will assess the scope and depth of the privacy protection rights of a citizen in your state.

Learning Objectives

Upon completing this lab, you will be able to:

- Relate state government data security breach notification laws to individual privacy.
- Explain why state governments have data security breach notification laws.
- Find a specific state's data and security breach notification law.
- Download a copy of a specific state's data and security breach notification law.
- Assess the scope and depth of the privacy protection rights of a citizen of any particular state.

Deliverables

Upon completion of this lab, you are required to provide the following deliverables to your instructor:

1. Lab Report file;
2. Lab Assessments file.

Instructor Demo

The Instructor will present the instructions for this lab. This will start with a general discussion about privacy law and how state governments implement data and security breach notification laws to inform their citizens that their privacy data has been compromised. The Instructor will then demonstrate the National Conference of State Legislatures (NCSL) Web site where a complete listing of data and security breach notification laws for 47 states as well as the District of Columbia, Guam, Puerto Rico, and the Virgin Islands are listed (three states have not passed legislation as of April 2014):

http://www.ncsl.org/IssuesResearch/TelecommunicationsInformationTechnology/SecurityBreach NotificationLaws/tabid/13489/Default.aspx

Hands-On Steps

> ▶**Note:**
> This is a paper-based lab. To successfully complete the deliverables for this lab, you will need access to Microsoft® Word or another compatible word processor. For some labs, you may also need access to a graphics line drawing application, such as Visio or PowerPoint. Refer to the Preface of this manual for information on creating the lab deliverable files.

1. On your local computer, **create** the **lab deliverable files**.

2. **Review** the **Lab Assessment Worksheet**. You will find answers to these questions as you proceed through the lab steps.

3. Currently, 47 states, the District of Columbia, Guam, Puerto Rico, and the Virgin Islands have data and security breach notification laws that define what organizations must do if they have had data or security breached that impact citizen privacy data. The National Conference of State Legislatures (NCSL) Web site tracks and organizes telecommunication and information technology state legislation. **Review** the NCSL Web site and data and security breach notification laws for each state listed at **http://www.ncsl.org/IssuesResearch/TelecommunicationsInformation Technology/SecurityBreachNotificationLaws/tabid/13489/Default.aspx**.

4. **Scroll** down the list of states and **find** the state of Virginia.

5. **Click** the **Va. Code § 18.2-186.6 link**.

6. **Review** the "Breach of personal information notification" law.

> **Reading Codified Law**
> If reading law text makes your eyes hurt, you are not alone. Legal text is jokingly known to be challenging to read, let alone understand. Statutory law is rarely written in a narrative form. Instead, it is very structured, if not formulaic. To make matters worse, a whole section might exist simply to explain a single prior word, for example, "redact" in the case of **Va. Code § 18.2-186.6**.
>
> This codified law is very structured and organized, laid out logically in nested divisions just as a software developer would develop "code." The increasingly narrow divisions start from the top as Titles, Chapters, Parts, Sections, Paragraphs, and down to Clauses. Each of those divisions can be broken into subdivisions, for example, a Paragraph of three Subparagraphs, with one Subparagraph containing 10 Clauses.
>
> Laws are broken down this way on purpose, to provide the reader clear, and clearer, definitions of a narrow topic. The best approach is to be aware of the numbering to know when you going deeper into a definition, or rising back out of one.

7. In your Lab Report file, **explain** how state government data security breach notification laws relate to individual privacy.

8. **Click** the **Back button** on your browser (or, if the Va. Code link opened a new window, **close** that **window**).

9. After you have returned to the list of states, **scroll** to find your state.

10. **Click** and **download** the security breach notification laws for your state. If you cannot download your state's security breach laws, return to the state of Virginia and use that information to complete this lab.

11. In your Lab Report file, **describe** the privacy protection rights that a citizen in your state has.

► **Note:**
This completes the lab. **Close** the **Web browser**, if you have not already done so.

Evaluation Criteria and Rubrics

The following are the evaluation criteria for this lab that students must perform:

1. Relate state government data security breach notification laws to individual privacy. – **[20%]**
2. Explain why state governments have data security breach notification laws. – **[20%]**
3. Find a specific state's data and security breach notification law. – **[20%]**
4. Download a copy of a specific state's data and security breach notification law. – **[20%]**
5. Assess the scope and depth of the privacy protection rights of a citizen of any particular state. – **[20%]**

Lab #6 - Assessment Worksheet

Identifying the Scope of Your State's Data and Security Breach Notification Law

Course Name and Number: _____

Student Name: _____

Instructor Name: _____

Lab Due Date: _____

Overview

In this lab, you reviewed the data security breach notification laws for your state and you assessed the scope and depth of the privacy protection rights of a citizen in your state.

Lab Assessment Questions & Answers

1. Were you successful in finding your state's data and security breach notification law? Specify the name of the law. If you were unable to download your state's law, use the state of Virginia to complete the question.

2. What is the purpose of state governments imposing a breach notification law on organizations to protect their citizens?

3. Explain how state government data security breach notification laws relate to individual privacy.

4. Assess the scope and depth of privacy protection rights that a citizen has by being a resident of a state. Write down the name of your state, and then identify the following for your state's breach notification law:
   - Who or what does the law in your state protect?
   - Does the law include both for profit and nonprofit organizations?
   - Does the law have a financial penalty assessed to the negligent party if proven guilty?
   - Does your state require the organization to publicly announce a breach to the media?
   - Does your state notification law take into account encrypted data or doesn't it matter whether the data is encrypted or not encrypted?
   - Does your state's law define the amount of time an organization has to publicly announce that a breach has occurred? If yes, specify the time. If no, describe how your state handles this.

5. True or false: If you are a citizen in one state but the company that had a data and security breach with your privacy data resides in another, the company must adhere to the data and security breach notification law of your home state.

6. Because most states have data and security breach notification laws related to their citizens' privacy, what is the number one reason for having these laws from a citizen protection perspective?

7. Some states define a data and security breach as the loss and exposure of citizen privacy data in an unencrypted manner. If a state encountered a data and security breach, but no citizen's privacy data was compromised given that it was encrypted in a steady-state within a database, does the company or organization have to abide by the data and security breach notification law?

8. True or false: Unauthorized access to a system must occur for the data and security breach notification law to take precedence.

Lab #7 Case Study on Digital Millennium Copyright Act: Napster

Introduction

If someone creates art, what is the value of the creation? How does the creator establish ownership of the art and protect that ownership? What is the government's role in helping protect that person's creation from someone else duplicating and profiting from it?

These are some of the questions to ask when discussing intellectual property and how to protect it. To help protect intellectual property, the United States used established treaties from the World Intellectual Property Organization (WIPO) to extend its own copyright law in the online realm. The result of that copyright extension is now known as the Digital Millennium Copyright Act (DMCA). The DMCA contains a significant number of provisions and exemptions.

In this lab, you will review the Digital Millennium Copyright Act and its provisions. You will also review a case study involving Napster, a company that violated the Digital Millennium Copyright Act.

Learning Objectives

Upon completing this lab, you will be able to:

- Describe the highlights of the Digital Millennium Copyright Act and its provisions.
- Relate the Digital Millennium Copyright Act to the Napster music-piracy case.
- Explain why Napster was not able to hide behind the defense of the Digital Millennium Copyright Act.
- Assess the impact of violations of copyright and the Digital Millennium Copyright Act from a legal, ethical, and information systems security perspective.

Deliverables

Upon completion of this lab, you are required to provide the following deliverables to your instructor:

1. Lab Report file;
2. Lab Assessments file.

Instructor Demo

The Instructor will present the instructions for this lab. This will start with a general discussion about copyright law and the Digital Millennium Copyright Act (DMCA). The Instructor will then present an overview of the DMCA and the case study.

Hands-On Steps

▶ **Note:**

This is a paper-based lab. To successfully complete the deliverables for this lab, you will need access to Microsoft® Word or another compatible word processor. For some labs, you may also need access to a graphics line drawing application, such as Visio or PowerPoint. Refer to the Preface of this manual for information on creating the lab deliverable files.

1. On your local computer, **create** the **lab deliverable files**.

2. **Review** the **Lab Assessment Worksheet**. You will find answers to these questions as you proceed through the lab steps.

Copyright Versus Trademark Versus Patent

This lab discusses copyright law. It uses the legal case against Napster, enforced by the Digital Millennium Copyright Act. But copyright is only one way to protect intellectual property. The other two are trademarks and patents. How do they differ? How are they the same? For as common as each protection is, understanding why one is used over the other is not as common as you might think.

The primary difference between a copyright, a trademark, and a patent is the type of intellectual property being protected. Other significant differences include for how long the property is protected, how to determine who wins if there's a dispute over ownership, and, basically, how to tell if the property is worthy of being protected.

If you write a song, produce a film, sculpt a piece of art, or write a mobile phone application and wish to protect it, then you will claim a copyright.

If you design a graphic, slogan, or symbol for your company and its product, then you would file for a trademark.

Lastly, if you invent a machine or design a special process, you may wish to file for a patent. A notable and recent change to how patents protect intellectual property is that since March 2013 the patent is awarded to the person who files first for the patent. This is a big change from more than 200 years of awarding the patent to the person who first came up with the invention.

3. **Review** the following case study on the Digital Millennium Copyright Act and Napster:

Napster was a company that used peer-to-peer networking to provide a file-sharing service that gave its users the ability to share music. The company existed only from June 1999 to July 2001.

In December 1999, the Recording Industry Association of America (RIAA) took legal action against Napster for copyright infringements. RIAA, the plaintiff, represented all major record labels in this action. It claimed that Napster violated "exclusive rights for reproduction and distribution of their copyright works." RIAA claimed that Napster made a "direct" infringement on its copyright and that it was liable for "contributory infringement of the plaintiff's copyright" and for "vicarious infringement of the plaintiff's copyright."

The law that stopped Napster from continuing its operations is the Digital Millennium Copyright Act that was enacted in 1998. The act addresses treaties signed in 1996 at the World Intellectual Property Organization (WIPO) Geneva conference and it contains other provisions. Software and entertainment industries supported the law, but many others opposed it, including academics, scientists, and librarians.

Following are key components of the act:

- It is a crime to circumvent antipiracy measures in commercial software.
- The manufacture, sale, or distribution of code-cracking devices used to illegally copy software is illegal.
- Copyright protection devices may be cracked for the purposes of encryption research, to assess product interoperability, and for the purposes of testing security systems.
- Under certain conditions, anti-circumvention provisions exempt nonprofit libraries, archives, and educational institutions.
- Internet service providers are protected from copyright infringement liability for the act of transmitting information over the Internet.
- Web site content that appears to infringe copyright law can be removed.
- Nonprofit institutions of higher education are protected from liability when faculty and students infringe on copyright.
- "Webcasters" must pay licensing fees to record companies.
- The Register of Copyrights, upon consulting with relevant parties, must provide Congress recommendations for "how to promote distance education through digital technologies" while "maintaining an appropriate balance between the rights of copyright owners and the needs of users."
- The act says that "nothing in this section shall affect rights, remedies, limitations, or defenses to copyright infringement, including fair use...."

4. On your local computer, **open** a new **Internet browser window**.

5. Using your favorite search engine, **search for more information** on the Napster case.

> ▶ **Note:**
> When developing your answers for the lab, try to remain objective and factual in your responses. Questions regarding whether actions by Napster or RIAA were justified are framed in the legal sense, not in the sense of any goodwill made from music sharing.

6. In your Lab Report file, **describe** the case and be sure to include the following topics:

- How did Napster try to defend itself against RIAA's claims?
- What does contributory infringement of copyright mean and how did this affect Napster?
- What does material contribution mean and how did this affect Napster?
- What was the court's decision about the case? What became of Napster?

7. In your Lab Report file, **describe** the provisions of the Digital Millennium Copyright Act.

8. In your Lab Report file, **explain** how the Digital Millennium Copyright Act affected the Napster music-piracy case.

▶**Note:**
Consider how the DMCA affects sharing of any intellectual property, not just music. Intellectual property can be anyone's idea or creation, be it art, music, an invention, or a book.

9. In your Lab Report file, **discuss** the impact you think this case study has from a legal, ethical, and information systems security perspective.

▶**Note:**
This completes the lab. **Close** the **Web browser**, if you have not already done so.

Evaluation Criteria and Rubrics

The following are the evaluation criteria for this lab that students must perform:

1. Describe the highlights of the Digital Millennium Copyright Act and its provisions. – **[25%]**
2. Relate the Digital Millennium Copyright Act to the Napster music-piracy case. – **[25%]**
3. Explain why Napster was not able to hide behind the defense of the Digital Millennium Copyright Act. – **[25%]**
4. Assess the impact of violations of copyright and the Digital Millennium Copyright Act from a legal, ethical, and information systems security perspective. – **[25%]**

Lab #7 - Assessment Worksheet

Case Study on Digital Millennium Copyright Act: Napster

Course Name and Number: _____

Student Name: _____

Instructor Name: _____

Lab Due Date: _____

Overview

In this lab, you reviewed the Digital Millennium Copyright Act and its provisions. You also reviewed a case study involving Napster, a company that violated the Digital Millennium Copyright Act.

Lab Assessment Questions & Answers

1. What was the premise behind the Recording Industry Association of America's lawsuit against Napster?

2. Based on your knowledge of how Napster worked, if you downloaded a copy of a song from a friend's hard drive using Napster, would you be infringing on the musician's or record company's copyright?

3. Describe the scope of the Digital Millennium Copyright Act and what or whom it protects.

4. What was the link between the Digital Millennium Copyright Act and the Napster legal proceedings?

5. What are the legal implications of Napster's online music-sharing service?

6. What are the ethical implications of Napster's online music-sharing service?

7. What are the information systems security implications of Napster's service?

8. Why did Napster ultimately have to shut down its services?

9. True or false: Napster obtained direct financial benefit from the infringement of users.

10. If Napster had acted as a distributor and provided back-end royalties through the RIAA to the original owners of copyrights to the music, do you think Napster would still be in existence and possibly one of the largest online music distributors?

Lab #8 Cyberstalking or Cyberbullying and Laws to Protect Individuals

Introduction

Cyberstalking and cyberbullying are not just terms for today's youth. They are real and increasing threats online. This is particularly true with social media, social communications, and social networking being done online. Protecting your identity, your privacy, and your data is a requirement for interacting and socializing online.

In this lab, you will define cyberstalking and cyberbullying and describe their legal implications, you will identify case studies for cyberstalking and cyberbullying, and you will define the requirements for a law to protect individuals from both of these threats.

Learning Objectives

Upon completing this lab, you will be able to:

- Define cyberstalking and describe the legal implications of cyberstalking an individual.
- Define cyberbullying and describe the legal implications of cyberbullying an individual.
- Identify case studies on cyberstalking and cyberbullying on the Internet.
- Define the requirements for a law to protect individuals from cyberstalking or cyberbullying.

Deliverables

Upon completion of this lab, you are required to provide the following deliverables to your instructor:

1. Lab Report file;
2. Lab Assessments file.

Instructor Demo

The Instructor will present the instructions for this lab. This will start with a general discussion about online social media, social communications, and social networking led by sites such as Facebook™, Twitter™, and MySpace™. A new breed of cyberstalking, cyberbullying, extortion, and blackmail has been created with social media, communications, and networking now online. The Instructor will then present an overview of searching the Internet for cyberstalking and cyberbullying case studies.

Hands-On Steps

> ▶ **Note:**
> This is a paper-based lab. To successfully complete the deliverables for this lab, you will need access to Microsoft® Word or another compatible word processor. For some labs, you may also need access to a graphics line drawing application, such as Visio or PowerPoint. Refer to the Preface of this manual for information on creating the lab deliverable files.

1. On your local computer, **create** the **lab deliverable files**.

2. **Review** the **Lab Assessment Worksheet**. You will find answers to these questions as you proceed through the lab steps.

3. On your local computer, **open** a new **Internet browser window**.

4. Using your favorite search engine, **search** the term **cyberstalking**.

5. In your Lab Report file, **define** what **cyberstalking** means.

6. In your Lab Report file, **describe** the legal implications of cyberstalking.

Stalking Is Stalking, Offline and Online

Even though cyberstalking might be new, the activity is well understood. Due to how technology changes so quickly, laws specifically tackling cyberstalking are new. In some areas, the laws might not even yet exist. However, the crime is already understood and dealt with by the law enforcement agencies ready to levy new charges.

Police appreciate the similar activity and analogous meaning between cyberstalking and stalking. The principal behaviors involved are harassment, intimidation, and incitement of hatred, etc. No one needs to reinvent a new crime definition, only new laws encompassing those behaviors online, as they sometimes include additional charges such as unauthorized use of a computer, mischief in relation to data, and, in school-age cases, child pornography. Of course, exact nomenclature of charges might vary by state or country, but the described activities are essentially the same.

7. Using your favorite search engine, **search** the Internet for a **cyberstalking case**.

8. In your Lab Report file, **describe** the case, including such facts as who was victimized and how the person was victimized.

9. In your Lab Report file, **explain** how you would protect this individual from the scenario presented in the case by outlining the law you would create.

10. Using your favorite search engine, **search** the term **cyberbullying**.

11. In your Lab Report file, **define** what **cyberbullying** means.

12. In your Lab Report file, **describe** the legal implications of cyberbullying.

▶**Note:**
As you consider the legal implications, reflect first on why a person might opt to cyberbully a person when they might not bully someone face-to-face.

13. Using your favorite search engine, **search** the Internet for a **cyberbullying case**.

14. In your Lab Report file, **describe** the case, including such facts as who was victimized and how the person was victimized.

15. In your Lab Report file, **explain** how you would protect this individual from the scenario presented in the case by outlining the law you would create.

▶**Note:**
This completes the lab. **Close** the **Web browser**, if you have not already done so.

Evaluation Criteria and Rubrics

The following are the evaluation criteria for this lab that students must perform:

1. Define cyberstalking and describe the legal implications of cyberstalking an individual. – **[25%]**
2. Define cyberbullying and describe the legal implications of cyberbullying an individual. – **[25%]**
3. Identify case studies on cyberstalking and cyberbullying on the Internet. – **[25%]**
4. Define the requirements for a law to protect individuals from cyberstalking or cyberbullying. – **[25%]**

Lab #8 - Assessment Worksheet

Cyberstalking or Cyberbullying and Laws to Protect Individuals

Course Name and Number: _____

Student Name: _____

Instructor Name: _____

Lab Due Date: _____

Overview

In this lab, you defined cyberstalking and cyberbullying and described their legal implications, you identified case studies for cyberstalking and cyberbullying, and you defined the requirements for a law to protect individuals from both of these threats.

Lab Assessment Questions & Answers

1. Define cyberstalking.

2. Define cyberbullying.

3. List the name of one of your case studies. Download a copy of it and insert the case study here.

4. Summarize your case study in one paragraph, highlighting the cyberstalking or cyberbullying scenario.

5. If you were to draft a law, what elements of that law would you include to protect individuals from the actions and outcomes occurring in your particular case?

Lab #9 Recommending IT Security Policies to Help Mitigate Risk

Introduction

The purpose of security policies is to help mitigate identified risks. Writing these policies is easier once you have created an asset inventory list, prioritized that list, and identified the major risk exposures found in those assets.

The task of identifying your IT assets begins with recognizing that your IT infrastructure and supporting resources can be divided into the seven IT domains. The benefit of identifying the assets and prioritizing them across those domains is being able to document policies in a systematic and thorough manner.

In this lab, you will create a high-level IT asset inventory list, you will prioritize those assets, you will identify the risk exposures, and you will make recommendations for policies that can mitigate the risk exposures.

Learning Objectives

Upon completing this lab, you will be able to:

- Create a high-level IT asset inventory list.
- Prioritize the IT assets in terms of importance to a school's operation and business.
- Identify the top five risk exposures found in the high-level IT asset assessment.
- Recommend IT security policies that can help mitigate the identified risk exposures.

Deliverables

Upon completion of this lab, you are required to provide the following deliverables to your instructor:

1. Lab Report file;
2. Lab Assessments file.

Instructor Demo

The Instructor will present the instructions for this lab. This will start with a general discussion about IT asset inventorying, prioritization and qualitative assessments of IT assets, and high-level risk assessment for those IT assets. The Instructor will then present an overview of the Family Educational Rights and Privacy Act (FERPA) compliance case study.

Hands-On Steps

> ▶**Note:**
> This is a paper-based lab. To successfully complete the deliverables for this lab, you will need access to Microsoft® Word or another compatible word processor. For some labs, you may also need access to a graphics line drawing application, such as Visio or PowerPoint. Refer to the Preface of this manual for information on creating the lab deliverable files.

1. On your local computer, **create** the **lab deliverable files**.

2. **Review** the **Lab Assessment Worksheet**. You will find answers to these questions as you proceed through the lab steps.

> ▶**Note:**
> Security policies mitigate risks in a wide variety of environments. Some risks are unique to different environments, and some environments produce highly significant risks. To counter these special environments, such as a hospital, school, or financial institution, the government legislates special acts to provide guidance and countermeasures. This lab uses the environment of a school and the guidance of the Family Educational Rights and Privacy Act (FERPA).

3. **Review** the following scenario for Premier Collegiate School:

Case Study: Premier Collegiate School

You are the new director for Information Technology at Premier Collegiate School. The private school teaches grade 7 through grade 12 with 300 students and 30 staff members and faculty. Each of the 10 administrative staff members has a dedicated desktop computer. The school's principal has a notebook computer that she takes home and when traveling to conduct both school business and personal tasks. She maintains a Facebook™ account and has opened a MySpace™ account to monitor the activities of the students who also have such accounts. The teachers have 10 computers that they share in the teacher's lounge to record grades and do all work associated with conducting their assigned classes (daily lesson plans, research, handouts, tests, quizzes, and final exams).

The school has two file servers. One is for administration business and the other serves student computing needs. The administration server has dedicated storage for each of the teachers and both hardwired access and wireless Local Area Network (LAN) access throughout the school. The student server has applications the students might need for their schoolwork, and provides wireless access for student-owned laptop computers. All students are required to have a laptop computer with wireless access. In addition, the

~~school has a dedicated computer lab with 25 desktop computers for the students to use in computer science classes.~~

4. In your Lab Report file, **list** the risk elements at the school.

5. On your local computer, **open** a new **Internet browser window**.

6. Using your favorite search engine, **search for information** on the **Family Educational Rights and Privacy Act (FERPA)**. This will help you complete part of the table outlined in the next step.

> ▶**Note:**
> FERPA differentiates between three types of information: educational information, Personally Identifiable Information (PII), and directory information. FERPA considers each with different levels of protection, especially with respect to disclosure.

7. The school's principal has requested that you prepare an IT asset list and a high-level prioritization or ranking of the IT assets given the function and purpose for administrative or student computing requirements. **Fill in the table** as follows:

- Based on your experience and knowledge of schools, **create** a comprehensive **asset list**. Keep in mind that assets include more than just physical objects you can hold. Do not forget that assets include electronic information, such as student records, lesson plans, test banks, and so on. Assets also include key personnel, such as knowledgeable instructors and important administrators.
- **Determine** the importance of each asset to the school function by **ranking** its placement on the list (starting with 1 as the most important, 2 as the second most important, and so on).
- Using Figure 1 that follows the table, **identify** which of the **seven domains** of a typical IT infrastructure each asset resides in. The data, systems, or applications may have student privacy data elements.
- **Perform** a high-level **FERPA compliance assessment** identifying where student privacy data resides and assessing the security controls protecting that data.
- **Prioritize** each asset by assigning it a Critical, Major, or Minor classification.

IT Asset Description	Ranking of IT Asset	One of Seven Domains	FERPA Privacy Data Impact	Assessment [Critical-Major-Minor]

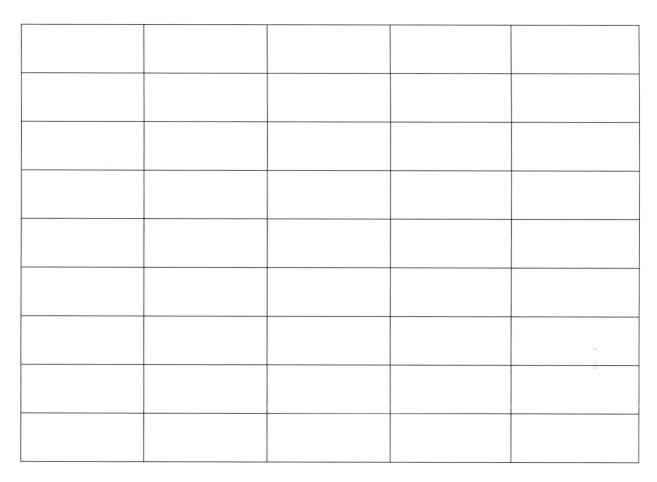

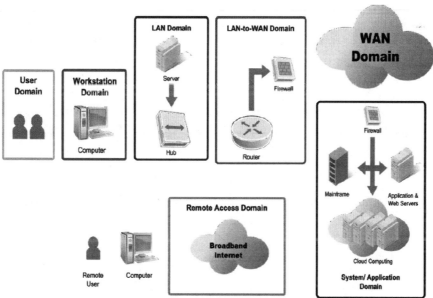

Figure 1 Seven domains of a typical IT infrastructure

> ▶**Note:**
> FERPA has no actual requirements specific to information assurance or security of student records. The act also doesn't contain a breach of security notification requirement, in a case where a school's servers holding education records are hacked.

8. In your Lab Report file, **list** three recommendations for **IT security policies** to help mitigate the risk exposures in the school's IT infrastructure.

> ▶**Note:**
> This completes the lab. **Close** the **Web browser**, if you have not already done so.

Evaluation Criteria and Rubrics

The following are the evaluation criteria for this lab that students must perform:

1. Create a high-level IT asset inventory list. – **[25%]**
2. Prioritize the IT assets in terms of importance to a school's operation and business. – **[25%]**
3. Identify the top five risk exposures found in the high-level IT asset assessment. – **[25%]**
4. Recommend IT security policies that can help mitigate the identified risk exposures. – **[25%]**

Lab #9 - Assessment Worksheet

Recommending IT Security Policies to Help Mitigate Risk

Course Name and Number: _____

Student Name: _____

Instructor Name: _____

Lab Due Date: _____

Overview

In this lab, you created a high-level IT asset inventory list, you prioritized those assets, you identified the risk exposures, and you made recommendations for policies that can mitigate the risk exposures.

Lab Assessment Questions & Answers

1. Which IT assets did you prioritize as critical to administrative or student computing?

2. List your top five (5) risk exposures for which you believe this school should have specific risk-mitigation strategies.

3. Given the potential risks that you identified, what IT security policies would you recommend that the school create to help mitigate each of the identified risk exposures you listed in question #2?

4. True or false: FERPA compliance law is about protecting students' privacy data, including personal information, grades, and transcripts. The law itself defines a privacy requirement but it does not specifically address security controls and security countermeasures.

5. Given that student privacy data is typically housed within administrative computers, systems, and databases, what can you do to mitigate the risk exposure that a student or someone on the student or school's network can access these systems?

6. For a school under FERPA compliance law, do you think the administrative computing or student computing network infrastructure is more important from a business and delivery of education perspective?

7. The school monitors the use of student social networking on Facebook™, MySpace™, and Twitter™. What should the school define and implement if it wants to define acceptable and unacceptable use of school IT assets, Internet, e-mail, and use of personal laptop computers on the school's network?

Lab #10 Case Study in Computer Forensics: Pharmaceutical Company

Introduction

During a criminal investigation, police might confiscate an object they believe was involved in a crime, such as a weapon or an article of clothing. They confiscate the object, document details about it, and keep it safe. It's important how the police handle the object in case the object is used as evidence for a trial. For a trial, it's important for the legal prosecutor to show the object is indeed the same object confiscated by the police. Police document their handling of evidence with what's known as a chain of custody. And the requirement is the same for electronic evidence as it is for physical evidence.

In this lab, you will look at the chain of custody procedures for digital evidence, review a computer forensics case study, and create a security incident response form to capture the steps needed to maintain chain of custody.

Learning Objectives

Upon completing this lab, you will be able to:

- Identify the key steps in maintaining chain of custody for digital evidence used in a court of law.
- Review a computer forensics case study and identify how and what evidence was captured.
- Relate chain of custody to a computer forensics case study for using digital evidence in a court of law.
- Create a security incident response form capturing the steps needed to maintain chain of custody integrity when responding to a security breach.

Deliverables

Upon completion of this lab, you are required to provide the following deliverables to your instructor:

1. Lab Report file;
2. Lab Assessments file.

Instructor Demo

The Instructor will present the instructions for this lab. This will start with a general discussion about the proper methods for handling physical evidence when trying to find digital evidence used as legal evidence. The Instructor will then present an overview of the pharmaceutical company case study.

Hands-On Steps

> **▶ Note:**
> This is a paper-based lab. To successfully complete the deliverables for this lab, you will need access to Microsoft® Word or another compatible word processor. For some labs, you may also need access to a graphics line drawing application, such as Visio or PowerPoint. Refer to the Preface of this manual for information on creating the lab deliverable files.

1. On your local computer, **create** the **lab deliverable files**.

2. **Review** the **Lab Assessment Worksheet**. You will find answers to these questions as you proceed through the lab steps.

3. **Review** the following computer forensics case study of a pharmaceutical company (the text for this case study originated at *http://www.evestigate.com/Case_Studies/Case%20Study%20Prescription%20Drug%20Diversion%20Brand%20Protection.pdf*; this case study can be freely distributed if no portion of it has been changed, including the following contact information: Toll Free: 1-800-868-8189; Int. Phone: Phone 727-287-6000; *http://www.evestigate.com*):

   (Global Digital Forensics—GDF—is a computer forensics consulting firm that is referenced throughout the case study below.)

   Global Digital Forensics Case Study Drug Diversion

   Case Type: Prescription Drug Diversion, Anti-Counterfeit, Brand Protection, and International Computer Forensics
   Environment: On-Site Seizure at Several Locations throughout the United States and Canada
   Industry: Pharmaceutical
   Systems Involved: Desktops, Laptops, E-mail, and Handheld Devices

   Case Background

   A pharmaceutical company began receiving complaints from its representatives in certain geographical areas that sales of normally high-volume drugs were slowing down considerably. The company's internal security department as well as the security departments of its major distributors began an investigation. The results of the investigation led the security professionals to believe a significant amount of the company's product was being diverted from foreign countries into the United States and sold through smaller distributors who specialized in sales to locally, privately owned pharmacies and dispensaries in nursing homes. The diversion activities were immediately reported to the local authorities in the regions as well as to the FDA.

An investigation was immediately launched and millions of dollars of diverted drugs and repackaging equipment was seized from several locations, including the warehouses of fully licensed pharmaceutical distributors. Along with the diverted product, the computers and other electronic equipment were also seized.

The seizure went smoothly and the company was satisfied as were investigators from the FDA and local law enforcement. However, the case was severely hindered by the fact that the majority of communications between the principals of the distribution companies (foreign nationals) and the foreign suppliers was conducted by e-mail. There were also no significant paper records on site. While the local authorities and the FDA had access to computer forensic labs, both faced similar roadblocks in their investigations. The labs were severely backlogged and the systems were encrypted, fairly complex, and recorded in a foreign language.

It became obvious that the investigation would be delayed until one of the labs cleared some high-priority cases and could dedicate the time required to forensically analyze the computers from the seizure. Time was of the essence. Everyone knew that the computer forensics had to begin immediately if the diversion was to cease and the case successfully prosecuted. Because the suspects claimed they were reshipping the drugs outside the U.S. (a legal practice) and had shipping bills that appeared to back this statement up, documentation from the computers was essential. If computer forensic analysis was delayed, it was almost assured that the U.S. Attorney's Office would drop the charges.

GDF Involvement

The company called in GDF and, working in cooperation with the local authorities as well as with the FDA and U.S. Attorney's Office, GDF was able to commence computer forensic analysis of the computers seized at the pharmaceutical warehouses and provide the information and artifacts recovered during the computer forensic analysis to the U.S. Attorney's Office.

GDF dispatched a Mobile Computer Forensics Lab and, along with investigators from the U.S Attorney's Office, created forensically sound copies of the hard drives seized from the warehouses to be used to conduct the computer forensic analysis. Strict chain of custody was maintained and the computer forensics was conducted under the supervision of the U.S. Attorney's Office following all accepted computer forensic methodologies.

The Findings

GDF Computer Forensic Specialists were able to decrypt and extract a wealth of information from the systems that were forensically analyzed. By conducting a complete computer forensic analysis of all the data the hard disks contained, GDF was able to provide documentation showing that the diverted drugs were being purchased from distributors in Europe and Canada and being shipped to the U.S.

in what appeared to be legitimate transactions. The computer forensic analysis also showed that the distributor had purchased equipment to unwrap the foreign drugs as well as repackaging equipment, all signs of a legitimate drug repackaging and exporting company.

GDF's computer forensic analysts were also able to extract documents showing that the owners of the distributors also controlled several pharmacies in the area as well as several nursing homes and ACLF facilities, all of which appeared to purchase drugs from the distributors. There were also many invoices for custom vitamins shipped to another distributor just two buildings away that appeared to be controlled by the suspects.

The Outcome

Using the digital evidence the computer forensic specialists gathered, along with the physical evidence, the United States Attorney was able to prove:

1. The distributor was purchasing drugs from foreign sources to be sold within the United States
2. The distributors were engaged in drug diversion for over 10 years
3. The distributor was repackaging vitamins manufactured to appear the same as the prescription drugs and selling and shipping them to Asia
4. The distributor was operating unlicensed pharmacies and nursing homes

The primary pharmaceutical company sustained over 13 million dollars a year in lost revenue. In addition, the suspects distributed millions of dollars in counterfeit drugs throughout Asia, potentially endangering the lives of hundreds of innocent people.

The suspects were convicted and sentenced in the United States and were being investigated in five other countries.

4. On your local computer, **open** a new **Internet browser window**.

5. Using your favorite search engine, **search** for the phrase **chain of custody for digital evidence**.

6. In your Lab Report file, **define** the phrase **chain of custody**.

▶ Note:
Mishandling evidence or improperly documenting the chain of custody can mean the difference between winning a court trial or the judge declaring a mistrial, and losing the case and legal costs.

---

7. Next, in your Lab Report file, **paraphrase** what you found for your search of **chain of custody for digital evidence**.

8. Using your favorite search engine, **search** for **security incident response form** to find examples of how and what data needs to be captured from one step or task to

the next to follow the proper chain of custody that includes sequencing and time/date stamp logging.

> **▶Note:**
> How well your team utilizes your security incident response form will determine how quickly the company can detect, respond, and recover from future incidents. One of the most important steps in security incident handling is the last step, which is "lessons learned."

9. In your Lab Report file and using the following table, **create** a **security incident response form** that captures the chain of custody procedures for the workstations, laptops, e-mail, and handheld devices for each individual in the case study. To follow chain of custody procedures, in the form, **address** the **individual identity or user of the equipment, model, make, serial number, operating systems, applications, and so on**. To follow chain of custody procedures, the form should also **answer the following questions** (each of these should be accompanied with a time/date stamp):

- What is the evidence?
- How did you get it?
- When was it collected?
- Who has handled it?
- Why did that person handle it?
- Where has it traveled, and where was it ultimately stored?

Security Incident Response Forensics Checklist

> **▶Note:**
> This form or checklist can be used for workstations and servers and other IT assets (for example, switches, routers, firewalls, and other assets) that have been affected by a security incident or breach.

{Example "Activities" are listed in the table.}

Initials	Date	Time	Activity
			Wipe, Partition, and Format TARGET Media
Serial Number:			
Software:			
Partition Notes:			

Initials	Date	Time	Activity
			Create Forensic Boot Disk

Notes:

Initials	Date	Time	Activity
			Verify Software License

License Information:

Notes:

Initials	Date	Time	Activity
			Physical Examination of SOURCE Computer

Location:

Make & Model:

Serial #:

Condition (On/Off, Damage):

Owner/User:

Notes:

Initials	Date	Time	Activity
			Source CMOS Examined

Clock:

Notes:

Initials	Date	Time	Activity
			Hard Disk(s) Removed (Unplugged/Prevents Booting from Source)

Notes:

Initials	Date	Time	Activity
			Hard Disk Information (how many?)

Number of Drives:

Make:

Capacity:

Serial #:

Bagged (Antistatic/Evidence Tape):

Name of Custodian:

Storage Location:

Notes:

Initials	Date	Time	Activity
			Description of Collection System From/To Imaging

Notes:

Initials	Date	Time	Activity
			Image Made

Software:

Details of Evidence Report:

Number of Images:

Notes:

Initials	Date	Time	Activity
			File Listing

Notes:

Initials	Date	Time	Activity
			Deleted File Recovery

Notes:

▶ **Note:**
This completes the lab. **Close** the **Web browser**, if you have not already done so.

Evaluation Criteria and Rubrics

The following are the evaluation criteria for this lab that students must perform:

1. Identify the key steps in maintaining chain of custody for digital evidence used in a court of law. – **[25%]**
2. Review a computer forensics case study and identify how and what evidence was captured. – **[25%]**
3. Relate chain of custody to a computer forensics case study for using digital evidence in a court of law. – **[25%]**
4. Create a security incident response form capturing the steps needed to maintain chain of custody integrity when responding to a security breach. – **[25%]**

Lab #10 - Assessment Worksheet

Case Study in Computer Forensics: Pharmaceutical Company

Course Name and Number: _____

Student Name: _____

Instructor Name: _____

Lab Due Date: _____

Overview

In this lab, you looked at the chain of custody procedures for digital evidence, reviewed a computer forensics case study, and created a security incident response form to capture the steps needed to maintain chain of custody.

Lab Assessment Questions & Answers

1. List the steps in maintaining chain of custody for digital evidence.

2. Why is it important to follow the chain of custody when gathering evidence?

3. For the computer forensics case, identify what evidence the forensics experts were able to gather.

4. Name two of the things the United States attorney was able to prove in the computer forensics case.

5. What important questions should the security incident response form answer?

6. Why is it important to include a time/date stamp in the security incident response form?